Hobby Farming

How You Can Grow Food, Raise Livestock and Making the Most of Your Space.

James Green

Introduction

If you're interested in growing your own food, caring for your own animals, or making the best of available land, then look no further than hobby farming! Farming doesn't have to be difficult and tedious work that requires dressing in dungarees and having access to hundreds of acres of land. You can be a very successful – even profitable – hobby farmer in an urban area with only a tiny yard to work with.

Hobby farms are generally small farms, but not all small farms are hobby farms. The technical definition of a small farm is one that generates less than $250,000 annually from its operations. That said, even a farm generating as little as $1,000 per year from its operations is still considered a farm. It's essential to keep in mind several hobby farms generate produce worth much more than $1,000. Yet, they aren't considered a small farm since they don't sell their produce or operate their farms as a commercial activity.

The best thing about modern farming is that it requires minimal attention and works great as a side project, potentially earning you extra money while you carry on with your day job. Now, as easy and accessible as it may sound, there are a few very important things you should know before planting or raising anything in your backyard.

Not only is it about efficiency and getting the most out of the effort you put into your farming endeavor, but it's about the safety of whatever you choose to farm and the surrounding environment. Even if you're considering a small vegetable patch to provide you with fresh strawberries and cucumbers, you want to do it sustainably.

Animal farming requires the ability to properly address the needs of the animals if you want to give them a good life and enjoy the many benefits of this type of agriculture. Invariably, like any other hobby or job, there is a right way to do things and a learning curve.

However, the most important thing about hobby farming is passion – and patience! Do you enjoy the outdoors and the farming lifestyle? This beginner friendly book will introduce you to the various farming areas, helping you approach them as efficiently and responsibly as possible. Whether you want to grow your own fruit or vegetables, or raise animals, the following s will give you all the fundamentals you need to get started.

What Kind of Resources Do You Have?

The first thing to understand is the environment that is immediately available to you. Study it carefully and assess it before you invest in it. Even if you aren't investing a lot of money to begin with, it will still take a lot of time, effort, and patience to grow a farm successfully.

You need to consider three essential agricultural resources that are land, water, and climate.

Land

For those in the open country with access to a few acres of land, assess soil quality and the ground topography.

Also, consider the "geological history" of the area. Has any crop ever been cultivated on this land? How long has the land been vacant? What is the condition of the land you are starting with? Is it completely barren, or is it a dense forest? Is it rocky terrain? These are all crucial aspects to consider if you plan on growing plants or farming animals.

In parallel, assessing soil quality and the nature of the terrain is just as important for urban hobby farmers looking to undertake something in their backyard. Without a proper evaluation, it will be hard to determine the nutrients you need to make the soil fertile enough to yield good quality growth. Sure, you could just plant a few seedlings and see how they do, but you will face unnecessarily high mortality and sub-standard growth.

If you're in an urban area, you could also consider indoor plantations or an indoor coop for poultry. Keeping things indoors does give you a high level of control over the environment, but it does require an even higher level of maintenance and can be costly to set up.

Water

Whether you plan on cultivating plants or raising livestock, water is a vital component in farming. It has so many uses around the farm that you can never have enough of it. Apart from hydrating crops and animals, you'll need water for spraying, irrigation, cleaning, and sanitation. It is highly recommended to have a water storage solution for your farm for emergencies. Not only should you make sure the water quality for your farm is good, but you also need to ensure that you do not impact the quality of nearby surface water sources (rivers, streams, ponds, lakes, etc.).

In an urban environment, you will probably have a water supply running to your home. Check the quality of the water you have available. Most commonly, water for municipalities is pumped out from deep-underground sources. Depending on how deep these sources lie, you could have crystal clear mineral water or unusable hard water. Urban water authorities generally treat water to make it safe for consumption through filtration and chemicals, but these processes can harm agricultural operations.

Ideally, if you have access to a bore and pump your own water, it's still a good idea to test water quality.

Some vast pieces of land have a natural water source like a nearby stream or reservoir. You will want to make sure there isn't anything contaminating the water upstream or around the reservoir.

Other than the quality of the water, quantity also matters. You must ensure that you have a consistent supply of water all through the year. Both plants and animals will require varying amounts of water at different times, so make sure you can accommodate those to guarantee consistent, healthy growth.

Climate

If you opt for the indoor route, this won't be a major consideration, but the climate is critical when creating an outdoor setup. While most cultivated plants are very resilient and can survive wide climatic variations, you don't just want them to survive. You want them to grow optimally.

Aside from temperature, it's good to know the average amount of rainfall your area gets, how many hours of sunshine, and the length of each season. This information will help you proactively manage your farm rather than rely on approximations and "eye-balling."

Most plants have a fixed season for when they can be planted and when they can be harvested. It's best to introduce animals to the farm at a time of year that provides them with the right temperature. This particularly holds true if you want to raise animals from a very young age. By contrast, if you adopt fully-grown animals, while they're a lot more resilient to climate, you will still need to have the right infrastructure.

How Much Are You Willing to Invest?

Hobby farming isn't just about money. Farming, in all its forms, is a timeintensive occupation. Of course, once you get the ball rolling, it won't require as much of your time, but initially, time is of the essence.

If you don't have a lot of time or don't enjoy looking after sensitive plants or young animals, you want to closely evaluate the choices you make. Things like strawberries, grapes, and baby chicks require a lot of attention and call for just the right environment for them to prosper. If you're lucky enough to live in an area that naturally provides the right environment for these sensitive beings, that's great. However, if your area is too hot or cold, it's still possible to farm delicate organisms, provided you put in the effort.

Planting a few seedlings out in your yard and watering them twice a week along with the rest of the garden will work, but it will deliver far from optimum results. Just throwing a bag of manure all over your crop will provide the soil with fuel to aid plant growth, but it isn't the best way to enrich the ground. Even small farm animals such as chickens and goats can survive on kitchen scraps and things, but they forage off the ground. Getting your animals in top shape and producing high-quality produce requires you to fuel them with what they need at different stages of their lives.

More often than not, the most important thing you can invest in your hobby farm is effort. Setting up a thermometer in the chicken coop to monitor temperatures is neither difficult nor expensive, but checking on it regularly and making appropriate changes requires dedication and effort. Many of the problems that small-scale (and even large-scale) farmers face have nothing to do with poor raw material quality. It's usually inadequate management systems and poor upkeep of the infrastructure that cause issues.

Large-scale farmers often complain that their expensive drip irrigation system has failed them, and that this technology is no good. The problem is investigated, and it is determined that the system had no periodic maintenance, the hardware was not cleaned and inspected regularly. A blind eye was turned to small clues that foreshadowed oncoming problems, and it is clear that technology isn't to blame.

With hobby farming, it's important to realize that plants and animals can take several months, even years, to mature. They'll require a high level of maintenance and care if you want them to develop into profitable assets. During this time, don't expect much from your plants or animals. The best you can get is a sense of achievement and satisfaction that you provided the farm with what is needed on that day. If you're farming larger animals like cows and growing fruit that grows on trees, it could be several years before you see any return. Be ready to commit long-term. Farming at any scale is not a weekend DIY project!

Teamwork

It's your farm, your project, and you'll be doing most of the work, but that doesn't mean you can be a one-person army. Depending on the scale of farming you want to undertake, you might need people to assist you or proper machinery to help you get the job done. If it's your first time getting into farming of any kind, it's best to start small. If you think you can handle 50 chickens because your neighbor is raising 35 in half the space, start with two dozen chicks. Like most things, it's quite easy to scale up your farm, but trying to manage one that is beyond your grasp can quickly become a nightmare. You will waste a lot of resources with poor management and neglect, and if you are farming animals, poor maintenance could cause disease and stress. This can quickly become a real hassle to manage.

Some of the people you want to develop good relationships with right from the start are plumbers, veterinarians, horticulture specialists, and the team at your local farming supply store. Let's say you want to have a larger hobby farm, with a plantation over ten acres or more, or home to more than a hundred animals. In that case, you may also want to connect with wholesale suppliers for everything you'll need and get a reliable truck as well.

Having the right team to work with will make all the difference between a high crop yield and an empty harvest. Contact with experts will give you access to valuable information and a wealth of experience, which is crucial for new farmers. If you can connect with local experts, that will be even better. Sure, you can find all the information you need online, but local experts will know the specificities of your area. They have hands-on experience, know the best varieties of plants and animal breeds available, and have solutions to remedy any problem. Not to mention the ease of access if you ever need to reach out to them on short notice.

Many of these local experts can be a great source for you in terms of acquiring products. Large poultry farmers often provide chicks, feed, and equipment for smaller hobby farmers. In the same sense, local growers can provide you with high-quality seed and essential starters for the plants. They can even suggest the best preventive measures for regional threats (bugs, locusts, and birds that visit the area seasonally).

What's the Goal?

Goals provide a pivotal point from which to consider starting your farm. Only with a clear goal in mind can you evaluate the kind of work you're willing to put into the farm and the kind of farm you want to create.

Brightening up a backyard with a few chickens and vegetable plants is quite different from setting up a dedicated vegetable patch and chicken coop. Most hobby farms are subsistence projects, meaning their farmers don't aim to sell anything at the local market. They simply aim to produce enough to feed themselves and their immediate circle. That said, should they have a surplus, they won't shy away from an opportunity to make some extra money. Having an end goal is bound to make the initial steps clearer. For example, if you're looking to produce eggs, you want a breed of chicken that is a good layer rather than one that only lays six eggs in a year. Similarly, if you're going to grow an exotic variety of lemons, you need to source that exact seedling for the best results.

So, decide on a goal for your hobby farm and work toward that with tunnel vision. As long as your goal is realistic, and you've conducted enough research to ensure its achievability, dedication and perseverance will take you far.

Growth

With all these aspects in mind, you'll be able to forecast a growth cycle and determine when certain tasks need to be done to achieve your targets. Ultimately, the kind of growth you will achieve as a hobby farmer is a combination of the product you choose to farm and how you go about farming it. For instance, if you specialize in poultry farming, your goal might just be to maintain a certain number of animals all year round and harvest eggs from them.

Working with the same assets, other people may choose to start an incubator and breed their own variety of chicken. They may also want to specialize in farming chicks as their sole focus.

People farming cows can raise these animals for milk, meat, skin, or just for the love of the animals.

If money and time aren't a problem, you're free to choose what appeals to you the most and manage it however you want. If you're going to make your hobby farming sustainable, it's important to plan your growth in incremental, manageable steps.

Now, let's have a closer look at the different areas of hobby farming and see how you can get started.

Tools and Equipment For Agriculture

Water Pumps

Water is, by far, the most used resource on a farm. Depending on where you're drawing water from or pumping it to, you may need a submersible pump, a monoblock pump, a grey-water drainage pump, or a circulation pump. Be sure to verify the kind of electric source you have and the exact size of the pipes you're going to be pumping through. This is to ensure the right pressure and gallon-per-minute flow for your crop. A water pump can be expensive, but it's a one-time investment. So, it's important to buy a good quality pump that will last and save you electricity at the same time.

Tractors, Trucks ATV's

On a small farm, you can get by manually tilling your land or using an engine-powered walk-behind tractor. That said, even a single full-size tractor can help you in your activities around the farm as it's very versatile and an ideal towing vehicle. Consider getting a truck or an ATV to transport material around the farm. Tractors, trucks, and ATVs can be fitted with different attachments and used for various purposes. Keep your farm's growth in mind and purchase (or rent) a vehicle that will be operational when your workload increases. This will ensure you don't have to invest in another vehicle later on.

Mowers

These machines are helpful for making hay, maintaining pastures, and readying new areas on the farm. Mowers come in various sizes and capacities depending on your workload, and you can fit them with multiple attachments to suit different jobs.

Backhoes

You can get hydraulic backhoes as stand-alone equipment or get them as an attachment for your tractor. There are different sizes depending on your applications and needs. Around the farm, there's always some kind of construction happening, and these are quite helpful to move rocks and boulders. They're also very effective for digging holes if you want to plant trees or create foundations for a structure.

Sprayers

Invest in handheld sprayers with a tank you can strap to your back and walk around your crop to spray pesticides, insecticides, compost tea, or any other kind of liquid. If you need to cover a larger area, you could get a sprayer attachment for your tractor with its own storage tank as well as a sprayer barrel. That way, you can just drive across the crops and spray them with what they need.

Irrigations Systems

As with most things around the farm, the kind of irrigation system you use will mainly depend on the crop you have and the farm area. You could use a soaker hose at a very basic level, which is a decent yet inefficient solution. If you have the budget for it, opt for a multi-level drip irrigation system - very precise and efficient but quite expensive. Because effective irrigation is the key to a productive farm, be sure to study the water requirements of your crop and create a solution that will meet those needs. Solutions like surface irrigation and high-flow sprinkler systems are also reasonable solutions. Ultimately, it depends on the kind of land you have and the crop with which you're working

As we've seen, water will also be vital for livestock. Even if you have a consistent water supply, it's always best to have water storage. Depending on the water quality, you may also consider investing in a filtration system to make the water completely safe for livestock to consume. The best type of water filtration will depend on the type of water you receive from the municipality.

If you're covering a large area of land, it's also a good idea to harvest rainwater. It's a source of clean water to be used for domestic purposes around the farm and at home. Even if you don't experience a lot of rainfall over a large area, one good heavy shower can produce thousands of gallons of water.

Scythe, Sickle, And Rakes

Cutting grass, weeding the fields, leveling out the land, and preparing the earth for planting seeds are typical activities for any farmer. The scythe, sickle, and rake are vital tools to get these jobs done, but they're only effective for small-scale farms. If you have several acres of land to tend to, it would be best to use a mechanical extension connected to a tractor. Depending on how you need to till the earth, you'll use different tools and their mechanical counterparts. Whatever the use may be, these are essential tools to have, and it's always wise to invest in more than one.

Harvesters

While harvesters are most frequently used for grain, recently, many harvesters have been developed to work for fruit farms and other types of agricultural produce. Again, this is one of those things that is done manually on a small scale, but harvesters have become much cheaper and are bound to be a worthwhile investment when you scale up. There are even harvesters available for sensitive crops like strawberries, so be sure to look around and find something that meets your needs.

Cultivators

Cultivators are some of the most important tools on your farm because they prepare the land for planting seeds. Whether you're running a small or large operation and regardless of what crop you're growing, you'll need a solid cultivator to prep the earth with. For small-scale farms, a two-handed walkbehind type of cultivator is a great tool that is both robust and cost-effective. In fact, cultivating the land by hand can be very labor-intensive and timeconsuming. Also, you won't get the results you would when using dedicated tools and machinery. Also, with machinery, you can ensure homogenous results all over the crop regardless of how large it is. In the end, if you start off with poorly cultivated land, getting good results will be almost impossible.

You can easily find cultivator attachments for tractors of all sizes and ones with all kinds of tips to prepare your land. More than just for tilling, cultivators can be a great tool to perform various ground-related tasks. So be sure to make this useful piece of equipment a part of your farming experience.

Plows

Along with cultivators, plows are also a highly used piece of equipment on the farm. You could go for manual plows, which are fine for small areas. For larger operations, you'll need a tractor-driven plow. In most cases, you'll need a variety of plows to get the job done. This largely depends on the kind of crop you're cultivating, the condition of the land, and the particular soil type with which you are working.

Among the different kinds of plows, some have interchangeable heads so that the base frame remains the same while the head that is in contact with the earth can be interchanged. Other types have a fixed body type, and, for this kind of plow, you'll need a different set to perform different jobs. Just like cultivators, there's a large variety of plows that suit every budget and requirement. Some of the most frequently used kinds include chisel plows and disk plows, but be sure to get the right one for your crop.

Harrow

These are used to level the soil, usually before it is tilled and readied for plantation. Harrows are driven by a tractor, and you can get different sizes to meet your needs. Most harrows have an adjustable setting, allowing you to get the right amount of surface compactness.

Transplanter

For certain crops grown from young plants and seedlings rather than seeds, a transplanter is a quick and efficient piece of machinery to dig small holes and plant plants. Typically, a transplanter is a stand-alone piece of equipment, and you can get manual versions that you can walk behind, as well as enginepowered models. If you have a tractor, there are also transplanters that you can attach to your tractor. Some transplanters can work independently with the tractor driver controlling them, while others require a dedicated transplanter operator.

These are some of the most commonly used tools and equipment found on hobby farms. As we've seen, how many you'll need and in what sizes will depend on your agricultural or livestock raising requirements. At the end of the day, it's a good idea to get machinery that's slightly larger or more powerful than you need. That way, you won't need to upgrade when you scale up and avoid finding yourself limited by machinery. With regular maintenance and good care (except disposable syringes and other ephemeral items), most of this machinery will serve you for many years to come.

Veggie Gardening

Gardening is one of those rewarding activities that let you enjoy what you love most and supplement your food reserves. While cultivating a garden can seem daunting, you can easily grow and maintain a healthy and thriving garden with the proper knowledge about beginner-friendly crops. This explores the best vegetables and herbs that you can consider for your small plot or home. When choosing a plot and seeds, there are many things to factor in, like soil type, climate, and season. Different types of farm produce have specific harvest periods. Without further ado, let's dig in!

Choose the Right Location

First and foremost, choosing the right location for your garden is of the essence. A poor place for your garden can result in substandard veggies, which is why you must consider the size of the space that you have in your garden or planting area. If you want to have a full-size garden, you need to plan it properly. Consider the following tips to get a good site for your very own vegetable garden.

- Sunny location: Your vegetables need about six to eight hours of direct sunlight every day. Very few types of veggies can tolerate shaded environments or generally low temperatures.

• Not windy: Favor a site that isn't characterized by heavy winds. Heavy wind can drive away pollinators, meaning they may not be able to complete their job. The place should also be stable and not prone to other weather whims such as floods or frost.

• Good drainage: Vegetables typically don't require a lot of water or poorly drained terrain where the water pools. In fact, continuously wet soil can lead to the rotting of the plant roots. You can use the strategy of planting your veggies on elevated beds. Simply make sure the soil is free of rocks since they can interfere with plant roots and affect their growth.

• Nutrient-rich soil: If you have poor soil, then you're likely to have unhealthy plants. To improve soil fertility, you should add plenty of organic matter to add nutrients to promote plant growth, as discussed previously.

Deciding the Size of Your Plot

Hobby farming beginners and enthusiasts should start with a small, manageable veggie garden. A large garden can become frustrating if you fail to manage your expectations. A common mistake to avoid early on is planting too many crops too soon or more than you want to consume. It is imperative to plan your garden with care not to waste your effort, time, and resources. Begin with something that you're comfortable with and that your family can consume.

A good starting point would be a space of about 100 square feet, then choosing three or five of your preferred veggies and trying them on a small portion. Ideally, try to create a raised bed that is manageable, and that helps prevent issues like water pooling. You can also design neat rows to enhance the free movement of human traffic without disrupting the vegetable plantations.

Choosing Veggies

Naturally, there are countless types of veggies you can consider for your garden. If you're entirely new to gardening, opt for vegetables that are easy to grow and productive. Before you buy your veggies, consult with an established farmer or local gardener to get insights into the types that grow well in your area. Certain vegetables that require cool temperatures may struggle to grow in your area if it's prone to warmness and humidity.

At the same time, start with vegetables that you and your family enjoy eating. Try to avoid over-planting, and check the availability of the veggies at your local market. Some vegetables are basic foods you should have at home, especially if you're a homeowner and have ample space to cultivate them. If you plan to travel for an extended period, say, during summer vacation, make sure someone is there to look after your garden.

Several plants require constant monitoring, or they'll suffer during the few days where they're left unattended. Cool-season veggies like peas, kale, lettuce, and root vegetables do well during cooler months. More importantly, you must use high-quality seeds to avoid wasting time. You may be tempted to buy cheaper seed packets in some cases, but these may fail to germinate. It's a good idea to settle for something that will produce better yields during harvest time. Here are some of the popular vegetables that you can consider for your garden.

Salad Greens

There are different types of salad greens that you can grow on your own. While lettuce and other plants for cooler climates save space, you can also grow them in containers. Plant salad greens in fall or spring, but make sure that the temperatures don't dip below freezing levels. With proper supervision and care, the plants should be ready for harvesting within 50 days.

Radishes

Similarly, plant radishes in fall or spring, as these generally take a few weeks to mature before you can harvest them. Radish plants can do well even in soil that lacks quality nutrients. It's best to pick the radishes when they're quite young so that you can use them for flavoring relish. Don't hesitate to use these plants in your compost if they grow too long and become inedible.

Green Beans

Green beans require less support to grow, so you should sow them after the frost when the soil begins to warm up. Plant the seeds about two inches deep in arid land and add compost to the bed to promote healthy growth. Keep the bed wet until the seeds sprout and spread out the watering days to allow the soil to dry. If you're growing pole beans, make sure they have enough support before they grow too big. The good thing about different varieties of beans is that they're easy to grow and maintain, aside from being very nutritious.

Potatoes

Potatoes are very easy to cultivate and can be grown in containers. If you get certified, disease-free seed potatoes, they take between 70 and 90 days to be harvested. Potatoes don't require hard labor since you only need to ensure they get sufficient moisture. You should also make sure that where you grow potatoes has good drainage, as the plants do not need excess moisture.

Ideally, they should be in a place that gets about six hours of sunlight a day. Come harvest time, simply dig up the potatoes from the ground.

Tomatoes

Who can imagine a garden without tomatoes? Fresh, homegrown tomatoes are very easy to cultivate and maintain. They can grow naturally from disposed of seeds when you prepare tomatoes for cooking. What's more, you can grow your tomatoes in containers or hanging planters, both indoor and outdoor.

These plants require plenty of sunlight and drainage to increase yield quality. Other plants can continue growing until they're killed by frost. You should test your soil first and get the right seeds, as tomatoes can take more time to harvest since they ripen during different periods. In any case, your garden will never be a failure if you choose to grow tomatoes.

Cabbage

Cabbage can be used for various cuisine and recipes, offering plenty of health benefits. Cabbages can grow larger, especially during summer days. Once you prepare adequately for this type of vegetable, it's quite easy to maintain. Opt for drip irrigation to retain sufficient moisture around the plant.

Carrots

Carrots are healthy and are used in a variety of dishes worldwide, from salads to smoothies. This type of root vegetable takes about 90 days to reach maturity. It's important to ensure that it gets enough moisture during its growth stage.

Miniature Corn

Also known as baby corn, you can include miniature corn in your veggie garden as it grows quickly. This cereal can be harvested when the stalks are still immature. Likewise, sweet corn is another non-vegetable product that you can grow in your garden. This crop requires a shorter period to be ready for harvesting.

Garlic

Garlic is used internationally and is renowned for its medicinal and seasonal properties. It's used for seasoning in a variety of dishes, and the good thing about the plant is that it is easy to grow. Easy to maintain, you can cultivate it all year round in different places with mild climates. Be sure not to overwater it if you want to get the best yield.

Sweet Potatoes

Sweet potatoes are pretty popular, particularly among healthy food enthusiasts. These roots are edible and are rich in carbohydrates and other nutrients. Their leaves are also used for all sorts of recipe ingredients. To grow sweet potatoes from the leaves, you need to create an elevated bed. There is no need to water sweet potatoes too often.

Peas

Peas will be a fantastic addition to your garden since they can provide vital nutrients to your diet. Growing peas only entails getting the right seeds to begin with. These crops need constant watering. Also, make sure that they're free from grass, which can affect growth. Other types of peas take about 70 to 90 days to reach maturity, and you can harvest them while they're still fresh. Simply make sure to refrigerate your harvest for future consumption.

Peppers

Various types of peppers can grow in your garden, all used for different purposes. The standard green, yellow, and red bell peppers are used in all sorts of dishes for flavoring and seasoning. While these plants are easy to maintain, you need to get the right seeds as well. If you're into spicy food, you can cultivate your own hot peppers instead of buying them from the supermarket.

Pumpkins

You can also grow pumpkins for special occasions like Halloween. If you grow more than enough pumpkins, you could sell the remainder at your local farmer's market. Pumpkins don't require a lot of water and should get sufficient energy from sunlight. Choose a cool, dry place to store your pumpkins to guarantee maximum freshness.

Baby Vegetables

As their name suggests, baby vegetables are tender, succulent, and extra tasty. There are different types of baby veggies to consider for your garden, including spinach, carrots, tomatoes, potatoes, and more. Other types include eggplants, cucumbers, leeks, and radishes. You should harvest these plants when they're still tender and fresh.

When to Plant Vegetables

Now that you have the right location for your garden and have selected your veggies, the next thing is to grow your crops. The process of producing a few tomato plants is simple and straightforward. However, if you intend to cultivate a full garden, there are several basic guidelines to follow. Let's dig a little deeper into the plantation process.

Timing

Generally speaking, all your vegetables cannot be planted at the same time. Specific crops like lettuce, peas, broccoli, and beetroots grow well in cooler weather, including fall and spring. By contrast, crops like tomatoes, cucumbers, and pepper should wait for warm weather in late spring or summer. Ideally, you need to grow taller plants on the northern side of the garden to prevent shading other shorter plants. If shade is unavoidable in your garden, you must reserve those spaces for cool-season veggies.

Some plants have a shorter maturity period, meaning you can harvest them earlier than others. For instance, green beans and radishes take less time to ripen, while plants like tomatoes have a longer maturity period. For that reason, it's essential to check the maturity time for each plant on the seed packet. All the same, you need to stagger the planting of similar seeds so you don't harvest them simultaneously. For instance, you can space out your lettuce for a few weeks to avoid harvesting it all at once. Other perishable crops may be difficult to store over longer periods.

If you intend to plant perennial crops or herbs, it's best to find a permanent spot in your garden where you can grow them. The climate in your area will determine when you can plant different crops in your garden. If you live in a cold climate with frost, get a calendar or conduct research to find the local frost dates. You also need to get information about planting, growing, and harvesting each crop in your garden.

Designing Your Garden

Putting together your first vegetable garden can be both exciting and challenging. When you design your garden, make sure you leave pathways to facilitate traffic between the rows of vegetables. Another important aspect is to locate your garden close to a water source. Alternatively, you can decide on the appropriate irrigation system that best suits the types of plants in your garden. Space the plants in each bed appropriately and make sure the crops aren't competing for sunlight.

Plant nutrition is also a crucial aspect since it helps promote the growth of your vegetables. For a small plot, consider organic manures that consist of natural ingredients. Artificial fertilizers made with chemicals can affect the taste and nutritional value of fresh vegetables. In parallel, pest and disease control should also be prioritized if you want to enjoy quality produce.

Lastly, but importantly, another aspect of gardening involves the need to rotate your vegetables - this will help maintain the quality and nutrients in the soil.

All in all, veggie gardening is a fantastic experience that enables you to supplement your food supplies while doing the things you love most. Before you set up your garden, finding the right location and choosing a sunny place is paramount. Keep in mind that vegetables require about six to eight hours of sunlight every day to increase productivity. Another important consideration is selecting the right veggies. As we've covered, there are countless vegetables you can consider. Try crops that you want to grow, but make sure they're compatible with the climate in your area. Finally, you must also ensure that your crops are free from disease, pests, and other elements affecting their health and growth.

Fruit Gardening

Are you wondering when the best time to plant your orchard is? You probably know that an orchard takes many years, if not decades, to thrive, but you can still grow yours today to enjoy its fruit in the coming years. Planting a fruit tree today is a superb future investment since you stand to reap the benefits for the rest of your life. In fact, no garden is complete if it doesn't have fruit trees. Planting trees from scratch may seem like a daunting task, but you're laying the foundation to get annual harvests for several years once you get started. This discusses the steps showing how you can plant and grow fruit or nut trees on the farm and explains how to keep them healthy until harvest time.

Location

First and foremost, choosing the right location for the orchard in your space is essential, just as with your vegetable garden. If you live in an urban area, you may face challenges like limited space, but this shouldn't stop you from planting fruit trees. Some trees naturally grow bigger than others, which can have a bearing on the quality of the fruit you can get.

Before you start digging holes where you want to plant the trees, it's imperative to plot the orchard layout on a piece of paper. You need to determine the dimensions you'll need to plant the trees. Provide an accurate scale on graph paper to figure out how many trees you can plant in a specific area of your garden.

Take into consideration the standard size of each tree when it reaches maturity. You can get this information from nurseries, or you conduct research online. Use colored markers to determine the space at your disposal to grow your trees. The size of the trees you want to grow also matters. You can choose between dwarf and standard trees, depending on the space available or the type of fruit trees you want to grow.

Another critical consideration is sunlight exposure (and its direction). Nut and fruit trees require plenty of sunlight, about six to eight hours per day, for optimum production. So, carefully choose the location for your garden according to your available sunlight. It's vital to understand the benefits and disadvantages of south-facing and north-facing slopes when you situate your orchard. North-facing sides usually enjoy mild temperature swings, which helps trees remain dormant for a longer period, protecting them against sudden temperature variations.

In parallel, keep in mind that open space may not be ideal if you live in a windy location. Heavy winds tend to blow away the flowers or even damage the branches with the fruit. If the tree is exposed to biting temperatures at night during winter, it may not provide the best harvest. Ideally, you must shelter your garden to protect it from strong winds.

Know the Type of Soil

As we've said earlier, the type of soil plays a crucial role in determining the location of your orchard. If the soil isn't appropriate for fruit trees, consider using it for another purpose to avoid wasting resources and space. Deep sandy loams with good under drainage are ideal for fruit trees. Ensure the loam soils are well-drained and that they harbor adequate nutrients to increase your chances of getting a great harvest. While soil pH varies from species to species, an average pH level of 6.0 to 6.5 is favorable for various types of nut and fruit trees. Other trees like blueberries require more acidic soil with a pH of around 4.5.

Be sure to take a sample to your local orchardist so that they can determine the suitability of your soil for tree growing. Very few trees except cranberries can tolerate wet and poorly drained soils. The issue with water logging or poor drainage is that they kill the roots and cause other inconveniences such as plant diseases. You can also inquire about the nature of nutrients that may be required for your type of soil. Practices like composting and using organic manures are highly recommended for fruit production, helping loosen the soil to facilitate water and air movement.

Know Different Types of Tree Diseases

Most crown and root diseases are caused by poor drainage, heavy soils, and waterlogging in trees. Spring thaw can affect the health of your trees in a variety of ways. The good news is that you can easily prevent this by creating a slope that promotes proper water drainage. Just like with vegetables, you can also use raised beds to plant your trees. Root diseases usually destroy the plant, and there is nothing to be done regarding the type of soil in those instances.

Other types of diseases, such as verticillium, affect brambles and straws and can be avoided by choosing a different spot from where the exposed crops were previously grown. Common types of crops affected by this kind of disease include melons, tomatoes, potatoes, peppers, and eggplants. In parallel, you'll need to understand the seasonal occurrence and the biology of different mites and insects that cause the disease. This will help you control the pests and maintain them at acceptable levels. A pest's life cycle details can help you select the best procedures to keep them at bay. Lastly, other pests and insects attach directly to the fruits. Fortunately, there are different remedies that you can consider to mitigate their impact.

Choose the Right Fruit Trees

Choosing the right fruit trees for your orchard is crucial. The good thing about fruit trees is that once you plant and it comes to maturity, it will give your exquisite fruit for several years to come. You can consider various fruit trees, like apples, peaches, pears, apricots, plums, and citrus. However, nut trees are different in that they can exceed 100 feet in height, spreading their branches to over 50 feet. While nut trees take several years to reach this stage, it's important to leave enough room in your orchard to avoid overcrowding.

While choosing your favorite fruit trees is essential, you should know that growing an orchard in an urban setup differs significantly from in a rural setting. Urban dwellers often lack the space and other vital elements to achieve the garden of their dreams. If you live in the city, you may consider fruit trees that offer benefits like successive ripening. For this, select different fruits that will ripen at different periods - this will allow you to enjoy fruit from your orchard all year long.

It's always a good idea to plant various fruit trees that belong to the same species in your orchard. Other plants require pollination from trees of cousin species. Trees that blossom during the same period can enhance the quality of your yield considerably. You can ask the people at the nursery where to buy your trees. When planting certain kinds of trees, you must exercise caution as some trees produce and emit chemicals that can impact other plants nearby. So, be sure to do your research first before planting your first orchard tree. Whether you purchase the trees from the nursery or online, you must get a clear description of each type. Certain trees can reach different heights upon maturity, which can impact other smaller species. Take into account that shorter trees shouldn't compete for light with taller ones in your garden. While pruning can also help you maintain the right size, trimming overgrown branches also helps promote healthy growth while maintaining the desired size.

Understand the Secret of the Fruit Tree

Not all fruit trees have the same characteristics that determine their growth. Some nurseries may not want you to know the truth about different types of fruit trees since they're concerned about their business interests. Some trees may never produce any fruit in certain climates, while others require what is known as "chill hours," which refers to temperatures ranging from 32°F and 46°F.

In most places, this corresponds to the period between October and February, while temperatures are high during summer. Because of this, you need to understand the nature of the climate in your area and use the internet to collect basic information about fruit trees. Bear in mind that some trees may not bear any fruit, especially in colder climates.

Layout the Orchard

After drafting the appearance of your fruit orchard on paper, you must perform the layout of the garden on the land where you want to set it. Avoid waterlogged areas and double-check to ensure that you leave ample space between the trees. Begin by establishing the corners of the garden and calculate your measurements from there.

Be sure to plant your trees in a straight line to optimize the appearance of your garden. Apart from improving the aesthetics, it will go a long way toward helping you harvest the fruit freely if your orchard is neatly designed. If you have a larger space that you intend to exploit for commercial purposes, plant the trees in rows with enough space to allow vehicles to move in between.

Tips for Tree Planting

It's imperative to prepare a proper hole that's about two to three times the width of the tree's root ball. When you fill the hole, the tree roots are surrounded by loose soil, making it easier for the roots to penetrate deeper. You can also use the fruit tree guild technique where other small plants are included with compost to fertilize the soil. The underplanting can provide mulch for your trees and help to retain moisture. These plants also attract insects that can pollinate the fruit trees when they reach the flowering stage. When you plant the tree, make sure the roots are below the surface. Remember that your trees need plenty of water for the first few days. Just avoid a situation where water-logging can develop as a result of poor drainage or hard ground. Also, provide a layer of protection against elements like cold temperatures during winter.

When to Plant Your Fruit Trees

If you live in a climate with hot summers or ground that freezes during winter, it's best to plant your trees in the fall. The issue with excessive heat is that it can affect the growth of a newly planted tree. Because of this, new trees need more water in summer, making it difficult for them to develop strong roots. The benefit of the fall season is that the fruit trees will follow a natural growth cycle where they'll be in a dormant stage, the ideal period to plant trees. Do not plant a tree on frozen ground.

Weed Management

Before you plant your fruit trees, you must ensure that the orchard is free of weeds. There are different steps that you can take to provide excellent weed management in your garden. Weeds have the potential to destroy your plants since they have greater resistance than other diseases. You must apply traditional techniques to eliminate grass since herbicides shouldn't be used for fruit production.

All you have to do is maintain bare soil during the first season of planting the fruit trees. Use a hoe to remove grass across the entire fruit orchard. You can plant a fall cover crop to protect the soil in August - this crop should be tilled or mowed off during springtime. The main benefit of cover crops is that it suppresses the weeds, limits winter heaving, and reduces winter erosion. It also helps harden the trees.

During the following years, you can maintain a strip of about one meter wide between the trees consisting of weed-free mulch. Weed control is vital in this place since it affects the root system of the trees and, ultimately, their growth. When your trees reach two years, you can grow a regular lawn sod throughout the orchard, except in areas surrounding the tree trunks. You can mow the lawn during the growing season and make sure you follow every step to manage weed growth for the first five to ten years. Then, once trees are well-established, they'll be able to overcome the grass. All you will need to do is trim the lawn to maintain a good appearance.

Fence Your Orchard

Fencing your orchard is an effective method to protect your trees against browsing critters. Make sure that the fence is about eight feet high to prevent stray animals from invading your plantation. Slanting the perimeter fence slightly outward can deter other animals that may be tempted to jump in. Alternatively, you can construct a fence around each tree, making sure to leave sufficient space for the branches to grow.

Weather elements can also threaten your trees. Because of this, you need to protect them when they're still young. For instance, you can erect a windshield or wrap the trees with plastic guards that protect against mowing. White fabric can also reflect heat during the hot summer seasons. When you choose to use a tree guard, make sure that it doesn't cause any damage. Each guard you use should leave enough room for ventilation and growth for your tree.

Fruit gardening is a superb hobby that will provide you with fresh fruit for several years. To grow a thriving orchard, you must choose the right plants and gather some knowledge about the type of soil in your area. The climate also plays a crucial role in determining the rate of growth of your trees. When you've established your garden, you should maintain it and ensure it's free of diseases. Prune all overgrown branches that can also affect the quality of yield of the fruit, and don't hesitate to bring in an expert should you encounter any obstacles or challenges.

Raising Chickens, Ducks, and Geese

So far, you've been learning how to grow and take care of fruit and veggies. Now it's time to take farming up a notch. If you genuinely want to be selfsustained, you've got to know your way around livestock and all types of it. In reality, taking care of livestock isn't easy. The good news, though, is that it is a simple job. This will explore how to raise and work with chickens, ducks, and geese.

Picking the Breeds

Purpose

Chickens: Egg-laying chicken breeds, such as Bovans Browns and White Leghorns, are lean and small, but they can only guarantee you an egg a day. Meanwhile, meat chickens like Cornish Cross chickens are generally bigger with more muscle content, and they grow faster, but they can't be relied on when it comes to eggs. Laying eggs requires a lot of energy, meaning the food can either go to the chicken or the egg. That said, if you aren't sure of what you want, or if you'd like a well-rounded choice that combines the best of both worlds, opt for dual-purpose chicken breeds, like Rhode Island Reds and Australorps.

Ducks: They're better egg layers than chickens because they don't need extra rest in the winter. Plus, one duck egg is equivalent to two chicken eggs in terms of size and nutritional content. Ducks also make great dual-purpose birds thanks to their full bellies, especially some breeds, like Buff Orpington ducks. If you want eggs, stick with Rouen and Magpies, but go with Muscovy and Pekin ducks if you want meat.

Geese: While their eggs are fewer (one egg every day and a half or two), they're much more prized. They're bigger than duck eggs and have over triple the nutritional content of chicken eggs. As for goose meat, it's delicious, highly prized, and will sell for more than chicken and duck meat. If you plan to sell them plump at Christmas, you'll find that Embden geese make a fine meat breed. Chinese geese are what you want if you're in it for the eggs more than anything else.

Nature

Chickens: To paraphrase what Forrest Gump might say, chickens are like a box of chocolates. They come in all temperaments. Some breeds are very friendly, others are shy, and others are aggressive - there's no general, onesize-fits-all description. The good news is, you can always train your chickens by establishing dominance - peck them back when they peck you. To sidestep the hassle until you've acquired enough experience, stick with guaranteed friendly and docile breeds, such as Australorps, Buff Orpingtons, and Cochins.

Ducks: They're the quietest and most docile of the three bird types. What's more, they can help you out by doing some good old pest control because they mainly forage for food.

Geese: They're generally loud, especially when threatened, making them an adequate choice for protection. They can also act aggressively towards newcomers and predators. They do form intense emotional bonds and get attached to their caretakers, though. In other words, treat a goose well, and you've got yourself a new friend for life.

Chicks vs. Pullets

After deciding on a breed, the next step is deciding whether you want to buy a chick or a ready-to-play pullet (a young female chicken - one-year-old or less - that is yet to start regularly laying eggs).

Chicks

The main drawback of buying chicks is the time and effort you'll need to care for them. If they are growing without a mother, you're going to need to assume that role. This means you've got to provide water, food, shelter, heat, and a safe space. In return, with proper care, your chicks are bound to grow up healthy, happy, and stress-free. By opting for newborn chicks, you'll be ensuring the purity of the breed you are raising, as well as proper husbandry practices. Keep in mind that your chicks will need a brooder (a small enclosure with a stable temperature, food, and water where they are kept until they're fit to care for themselves). While it can be expensive, a brooder is more of an investment, given that you'll be reusing it with the rest of your hatchlings to come.

Pullets

Pullets don't require much effort because they come ready to lay. All you've got to do for a pullet is provide them with food, water, and shelter. Here's the catch, though. Introducing a pullet to your flock can be rather difficult. First off, some pullets come with contagious diseases, such as fowl paralysis (Marek's disease), avian pox, and bronchitis. Unless you want to jeopardize the entire flock, you need to quarantine the infected birds until they've fully recovered, which can take about four weeks. Once you've confirmed the pullets are healthy, you'll need to gradually introduce them to the rest of your flock to avoid any fights or injuries. Chickens, ducks, and geese are pretty territorial. If a goose is willing to take on a fox to defend its territory, it won't think twice before going after a new pullet.

To sum up, if you're a first-timer, pullets are a great option because you'll get a little practice before dealing with delicate hatchlings. Plus, they're perfect for steady egg production. On the other hand, chicks are a little harder to care for, but you'll be able to pull it off without a doubt. That said, you won't be getting your eggs right away.

How Many Birds Do You Need?

There are three factors to consider when determining how many chicks to buy: zoning regulations, resources, and egg production.

Zoning Regulations

Unfortunately, you can't simply buy a couple of geese and just keep them around. Nowadays, everything is much more regulated. Each state and city have a specific limitation on the number of birds you're allowed to keep. In the United Kingdom, you can keep up to 50 without registering. In Italy, there are no regulations. In the U.S., you're free to do what you want in New York

City, whereas your limit is four in Wisconsin. Some municipalities also require building permits for coops, so be sure to check with the local authorities.

Resources

Before you bring in any number of chicks, you've got to make sure you have enough money to care for them as they grow older. Not just that, but you must also consider the size of your property. For mature chickens, you need at least 2 square feet per bird in your coop. For mature ducks, you'll need at least 3 square feet per bird. Geese, however, need 8 square feet per bird to be comfortable. If you don't have space, opt for a smaller flock to avoid overcrowding and territory fights.

Egg Production

You should also consider the number of eggs you want to end up with.

Healthy chickens and ducks lay one egg a day, except during molting season. This production rate can also decrease due to stress, lack of nutrition, and cold weather. Meanwhile, geese take one to two days to lay one egg. Are you planning on making money off of selling the eggs? Or do you intend to use the eggs for your own consumption? While your resources will dictate the size of your flock at first, your end game will decide whether you should expand.

Hatchlings

While mature birds simply need you to provide for their basic needs, hatchlings require much more care and attention to survive. They're very fragile, especially when without a mother.

Chicks

Temperature: Before your chicks arrive, you need to prepare a brooder. You can acquire one or make one using a cardboard/plastic box or an unused bathtub big enough to provide 2 square feet per chick. The brooder should be placed in a room or space where the temperature can be controlled. Especially in the first two weeks, the temperature should be kept at a minimum of 90°F/32°C. Otherwise, you'd risk the fluffy babies dying. At the 3-week mark, if your chicks are grown enough to fly out of their brooder, you can allow them outside for a short while only if it's warm enough (at least 70of and not windy). That said, remember always to keep them contained (any type of housing will do) and never to leave them unattended.

Using a heat lamp or a heating plate (highly recommended), you want to keep the temperature at 95°F/35°C during the first week, then decrease it by 5°F/3°C each week. By the end of the brooding period (4-5 weeks), they should have grown their feathers, which helps them regulate their body temperature. It's very common to find that some chicks develop faster than the rest, hence needing less heat. That's why it's important to create a temperature gradient. To do so, simply place the heat lamp over the brooder, not inside. If you're using a heating plate, place it in the brooder, but allow for plenty of space around it. Either way, don't forget to keep an eye on your chicks. If they're constantly crowding the heat source, it means they're too cold. If they often gather to the sides of the brooder, they're probably too hot.

Food and Water: Chicks require a specific set of nutrients at first, so you need to buy them chick starter feed. Note that if you haven't vaccinated them against coccidiosis, you must give them medicated feed (it contains Amprolium that helps chicks develop immunity). Fill up your feeder and let them go crazy, which they won't because birds stop eating when they're full. As for water, chicks need it right away, so make sure they know where it's located by guiding one chick towards the waterer and gently dipping its beak in the water. The others will follow the first chick, or you'll need to repeat the process with the lost ones.

Ducklings & Goslings

The same principles apply here - you need a brooder, a particular type of feed, and water, but the specifics are slightly different.

Living Space: They need the same amount of space as chicks but require more bedding (2 inches) because ducklings and goslings are considerably messier. Ideally, you want to use pine shavings for all your birds while keeping the bedding as dry as possible. With baby ducks and geese, you might have to change the bedding a couple of times a day rather than the typical once-a-week habit. Last but not least, never use newspapers. It's a slippery surface that can cause a deformity known as splayed or spraddle leg.

Temperature: Unlike chicks, these birds require less heat, which means a starting temperature of 90°F/32°C and a regular weekly decrease of 5-7°F/34°C.

Food and Water: While duck feed is ideal, chick starter feed (crumble, not powder) will work just fine for the first three weeks of a duckling or gosling's life, but you must make sure it isn't medicated. While medicated feed can be good for unvaccinated chicks, it could potentially harm the other birds. Either way, it's best to stay away from unnecessary chemicals whenever you can. These birds also require more niacin (vitamin) than chicks. If using chick feed, you'll need to supplement the water with niacin tablets (150mg/gallon) or sprinkle brewer's yeast on your feed (1.5 tablespoons per 1 cup of feed).

Water is just as important for ducks and geese, but they'll want to dip themselves fully in the water. At such a young age, they're prone to chilling (getting too cold). What you need to do is provide them with water deep enough so they can dip their heads and beaks into it, but keep it low enough so that they can't submerge their entire bodies.

Diet

Once your little birds grow up and start eating anything other than chick feed, you need to introduce grit (coarse sand) into their diet to help them digest the food since they don't have teeth. You can either mix it with the food or place it in a separate feeder. Birds usually find it naturally when foraging, but you'll need to provide it with your food. Other than that, feeding birds is as simple as reading the instructions on your feed bag. Don't hesitate to ask for recommendations from a seasoned farmer.

Chicken

After transitioning all your chicks from starter to grower feed (after the duration specified on your starter feed bag), a chicken's purpose will decide its feed type.

Layers: When they start laying their first eggs, but not before 20 weeks old, switch your layers to grower feed containing 18% protein and higher calcium.

Meat Chicken: Switch your meat chicken to 20% protein grower feed right away to help them grow large fast.

Ducks and Geese

The instructions here are the same for layers and meat birds. Essentially, you can use chicken feed for your ducks and geese, too, but you've got to remember the niacin. Growing birds require the same amount of niacin they needed in their first weeks until they're 20-weeks of age. That's when you should dial it back to half the amount. But don't give them bread, as it occupies space in their stomach without providing any nutrients. This prevents birds from eating enough feed, causing bone deformities and all types of physical development issues.

Breeding

In all cases, nature will do its job just fine. You just need to pick the best of your female birds to mate with a male with many desirable traits to ensure the best results. Apart from that, your job is to make it easy for the birds to breed, and it works the same way for all species, with a few exceptions.

Chickens

- Limit yourself to one rooster in the flock at first to avoid competition between roosters, as they'll get aggressive. A ratio of 1 (rooster):4-5 (hens) should be enough.
- Leave the rooster with the chosen hens, yet keep an eye on them, and don't worry if things get aggressive. You should keep in mind that some roosters can get a little rowdy, sometimes to the extent of drawing blood. When you find yourself with an over-eager rooster, simply separate him from the flock and reintroduce him once he's calmed down.
- For two weeks after mating, your chickens will be laying fertile eggs. To

differentiate between fertile and non-fertile eggs, the fertile ones look opaque when examined over a light. The yolk will also appear to have a red clump right in the middle.

- When you've collected the first fertilized eggs, simply store them for a week in the fridge until you've collected the rest, but keep the temperature between 50-55°F/10-12.7°C. Store them round-side up, making sure to rotate them gently every day. When you've collected all the eggs you want, put them all in the incubator. The reason behind storing fertile eggs is that opening the incubator while it is heating can damage the developing eggs.

Ducks and Geese

- These birds prefer to mate in water. A pond is a great option, but they won't say no to a kiddy's pool. If you choose to use a kiddy's pool, be sure to change the water regularly.
- The ratio of drakes to ducks should be 1:5-8. The ratio of gander to geese should be 1:3-5.
- Ganders should be mated about a month before the breeding season as they tend to take longer in the selection process.

Collecting and Storing Eggs

- Collect eggs early in the morning and check again during the day. Birds might accidentally damage their own eggs.
- While you're at it, make sure to clean up the nest boxes and remove the solid straws.
- After gathering, clean the eggs, preferably with a dry sponge.
- When done, pack and store the eggs in the refrigerator.

They should last for about a month.

Raising Cattle and Pigs

Millions of homesteaders raise cattle and pigs, be it for fulfilling dairy needs or for meat. Animal agriculture is an efficient way to harvest milk and to produce animal meat and animal-derived foods. As a hobby farming enthusiast looking for an endless supply of milk, cheese, yogurt, beef, and pork, this will walk you through the basics of raising cattle and pigs, including how to feed and breed the animals, how to decide the best breeds for use, and step-by-step instructions on how to create a pigpen. This is divided into two parts, illustrating the information on cattle and pigs separately. We'll also be differentiating between dairy cattle and beef cattle, specifying how to treat and care for the animal to ensure yourself a healthy harvest.

Raising Cattle

Cattle farming has been practiced since ancient times, dating as far back as 9000 CE. Milk is known to be the oldest and most complete animal food. This is why milk consumption has been a part of human history and culture for thousands of years. Owning cattle means you don't need to spend on dairy products like butter, cheese, cream, and yogurt. What's more, cattle can be used to produce beef and cultivate seed stock. With all the right resources, raising cattle can be a rewarding and profitable enterprise. However, to set up a satisfying enterprise, you must understand the key differences between dairy and beef cattle, the requirements to raise cattle, what breeds to choose, and how to care for the cattle.

Difference between Dairy and Beef Cattle

For starters, you may have noticed the broad spectrum of colors that cattle come in. Although they might look the same to non-experts, beef and dairy cattle have substantial differences. If you pay attention to their body type, beef cattle tend to be fleshier than dairy cattle. The beef cattle also tend to have more fat and muscles covering their body than an average dairy cow. They're stockier and often taller than dairy cattle.

You'll find dairy cattle to be fairly more angular, with larger and fuller mammary glands between their legs. For hundreds of years, dairy cow breeds have been crossed to obtain large amounts of milk. It is common for dairy cattle to produce more milk than what their calves need. That said, beef cattle are more heat tolerant than dairy cattle and can sustain hotter temperatures. On the other hand, dairy cattle need cooler temperatures and are best farmed in regions with moderate rainfall. Now that you have understood the main differences between beef and dairy cattle, let's discuss the different cattle breeds and how to select the best breed for your farm.

Types of Cattle Breeds

Whether you wish to breed cattle for dairy or beef, you'll find various cattle breeds to choose from. In the United States, there are about six major cattle breeds. The Holsteins and the Jerseys are the most commonly found breeds of dairy cattle, and their wide use in commercial dairy farming makes these two breeds easily available across America. Apart from the black-white Holsteins and the brown Jerseys, other major dairy cattle breeds in the United States include Ayrshire, Brown Swiss, Guernsey, and Milking Shorthorn. Dualpurpose cattle breeds such as the Dexters, the red-white variation of Holsteins, and miniature Jerseys are also considered novel dairy cattle breeds. If you want to raise cattle specifically for beef, it's essential to know that beef cattle breeds are generally classified into three types. Cow breeds (also known as maternal breeds), and the sire breeds (also known as terminal breeds), are the two main beef cattle breeds. The third type of beef cattle breed is a mix of the maternal and terminal cattle breeds – called the *composite breeds*. Maternal breeds generally have a moderate build and are known to raise healthy calves. Terminal breeds, on the other hand, are slightly larger and are typically used for meat production. Composite breeds are bred to adjust to specific environments and are known for their highquality pedigree.

Among the maternal breeds of beef cattle, Hereford, Shorthorn, Angus, and Red Angus are the most common in the United States. If you decide to raise terminal breeds of beef cattle, then breeds such as Simmental, Gelbvieh, Limousin, Charolais, and Maine Anjou will serve you the best. The most common composite breeds include Beefmaster, Bradford, Limflex, Maintainer, and the SimAngus breed.

Tips for Cattle Selection

If you have little experience buying cattle, the process of selection can be overwhelming. Selecting the best cow out of a herd requires practice and experience. Quite often, beginners in cattle farming end up buying an unhealthy cow prone to behavioral problems when milked, lower milk quality, or early death. To help you avoid these problems, here are a few tips that seasoned homesteaders have found useful while selecting their cattle.

1. Animal Performance

While selecting your cattle, you must first assess the animal's performance by evaluating some measurable traits. General information about the cattle, such as yearling weight, weaning weight, birth weight, and meat yield quality, can help assess how well a calf can grow. This information makes the selection process more straightforward.

2. Lameness

Lameness is the most common issue cattle suffer from. It's a painful problem that can arise for various reasons and lead the cattle to go lame. The reasons may include bacterial infection, poor nutrition, prolonged standing on lowquality or concrete floors, and inefficient foot trimming. If the cattle are limping, they may have serious problems like digital dermatitis, hoof lesions, laminitis, or sole ulcers.

3. Mastitis

Cattle often suffer from a chronic bacterial infection known as mastitis. It causes inflammation in the cattle's mammary glands and can be very difficult to cure. You can check for mastitis in a cow by feeling its udder. It shouldn't feel hot or hard to the touch, and the cow shouldn't flinch when you touch it. That said, missing teats and flakes in the milk can also be a sign of mastitis. Bearing this in mind, it's best to avoid these cattle.

4. Temperament

One of the most important characteristics to examine in some cattle is their temperament. If you're selecting dairy cattle, you should be even more careful. The cow must stay calm when getting milked. You should observe the way a cow behaves when you approach it. If you see signs of aggressiveness when you're milking it or if it avoids you when you approach, you'd probably do well without it in your barn.

5. Visual Appraisal

Most commercial producers use the visual aspects of an animal to evaluate appraisal. The structural aspects of the animal-like muscles, body capacity, ear shape and length, breed character, color distribution, and structural correctness helps with the visual appraisal. Evaluating the animal's visual appraisal helps producers identify defects that may not be clearly visible during performance evaluation.

How to Raise Cattle

Raising dairy and beef cattle requires you to be prepared with the necessary facilities. If you're planning on breeding, then you must have appropriate housing and fencing arrangements. A cow can drink around 45 gallons of water a day, which is why a sufficient clean water supply is so important. You should take an honest look at your land and determine whether the pasture-to-cow ratio will satisfy their needs; then, make adjustments accordingly.

Housing

Due to their large sizes, cattle require a lot of space to sit comfortably. Most of the time, cattle are tethered indoors with an iron chain or harness, and because of this, you must provide suitable indoor housing for your cattle. Good design and proper housing management go a long way in animal welfare. By protecting your cattle from inclement weather, high humidity, crowded conditions, and poor ventilation, you can decrease the chances of infections, diseases, and injuries.

Food

Cattle love grazing in lush green fields. Pastures are their natural habitats where they have complete freedom and opportunity to graze. The grass and vegetation that cattle survive on are filled with fiber. Cattle may also need nutrient-rich mixtures along with the forage to provide a high yield of milk. Cattle must have a good balance of fiber and nutrients in their diet for high performance.

Water

As stated above, to raise healthy cattle, you'll need a supply of clean and fresh water available at all times. Water is probably the most crucial part of their nutrition. Poor quality water or an inadequate amount of it can severely impact the cattle's food intake. It can also result in chronic diseases and decrease the animal's performance. You can supply clean water to your cattle in many ways using troughs, buckets, or an automatic watering system.

How and When to Breed Cattle

The breeding of cattle takes place specifically to increase the production of meat and milk. When a cow gives birth to a calf, it can produce large quantities of milk for around ten months. So, cattle should be bred annually. If the newborn is a heifer (female) calf, it's raised as dairy cattle, whereas, if it's a bull (male) calf, it may be raised as a beef cattle. Typically, dairy cattle can produce a high milk yield for an average of 2-3 years. Once the cattle can no longer produce enough milk, it's transported to a slaughterhouse and used for beef.

Raising Pigs

Pigs are one of the easiest animals to raise and breed. They grow faster than beef cattle and require far less commitment. That said, pigs provide significantly more meat than poultry animals. Raising pigs can help your farm become more self-sustainable. If you're planning to raise pigs to sell their meat, use them to supply good pork and delicious bacon. To keep them as pets, you'll need a place to house and care for them. It's easy to build a pigpen to keep your pigs. The following section will help you do it yourself the right and easy way.

How to Build a Pigpen

Allot a Space

Pigs need a dry place big enough for them to move about and protect them from weather conditions. It's believed that an average-sized pig only requires about 20-30 square feet of space. By contrast, a fully grown and healthy pig should be allotted at least 50 square feet of space. While planning the pigpen, another important thing to remember is that these animals tend to excrete near water bodies. Try to place the water supply as far away from their shelter and food as possible.

Build a Fence Around the Pen

After allocating appropriate space for the pigs, you'll need to build a sturdy wooden fence around the area. To make it stronger, you can attach welded wires to the inside of the wooden fence, helping to stabilize the fence if the pigs push on it. Some pigs also tend to dig under the fence to find a way out, but you can discourage this behavior by putting a hogtied board (excuse the pun) across the bottom of the fence. If you're going to let your pigs out of the pigpen often, it's best to invest in a movable electric fence.

Provide a Shelter

Your pigs will need protection from direct sunlight and bad weather. You must put a shed in at least one section of the pigpen, allowing the pigs to rest in the shelter of the shed in scorching heat and bad weather. You may place hay in the pigpen for colder weather so that piglets can keep themselves warm. It's best to install a three-sided roofed structure within the fenced area.

Put a Mud Wallow

Generally speaking, it's difficult for pigs to regulate their body temperature. This is why pigs tend to love mud, as it helps them cool down. You can easily put a mud wallow in the pigpen. All you need to do is dig up a section of the pen and fill it with water. You can then build a low-lying fence to restrict the water within the mud bath. Add water to the dug-up section once or twice a day.

Collect the Manure

Pigs produce a lot of manure every day, and you'll need to figure out how to utilize this. If you don't clear the manure from the pigpen, you might have to deal with swarms of flies. A fully grown pig can produce up to 1.6 pounds of manure in a single day. This manure can be used as a fertilizer for your crops or garden. You can also sell it to other gardeners or farmers in your locality.

How to Raise, Feed, & Care for Pigs

If you're planning to raise pigs, you should know that pigs grow best during summertime. If you start raising a 50-pound piglet in early spring, it can grow up to 250 pounds in just three months. When you acquire a piglet, select a healthy one from a trusted breeder. It's best to search nearby pig farms in your area. Try to avoid pigs that cough or scratch themselves. By assessing the other pigs on the farm you're buying from, you can determine whether the pig you're buying is actually healthy.

Pigs drink and eat in astonishing amounts. An average pig should get at least 2 to 4 gallons of water to drink and gain at least 1 lb. in a day to stay healthy. You can keep a water tub in the pigpen. Fix it to the ground to avoid spilling when the pigs drink from it and regularly fill it with fresh and clean water. To ensure that your pigs have a balanced diet, plan to feed them premixed feeds. If your piglet weighs 50 pounds, the diet must include 16% protein to promote growth. For a grown pig, 14% protein in the diet will suffice.

Lastly, pigs are prone to bacteria and internal parasites due to their tendency to rest in mud and excrete near water bodies. Thus, you must ask a local vet to prescribe anthelmintics for your pigs. These will help kill off any worms that your pigs might have. This treatment must be followed every four to six weeks.

Raising Sheep and Goats

If you want to raise sheep and/or goats, there are several things you must consider before you begin. For starters, you need to decide whether you want just sheep, just goats, or a mix of both. You also need to figure out your purpose for raising them. They both have their benefits, and you can use the things they produce either for yourself or to sell. This will cover some basic tips on how to get started with raising sheep and goats.

How to Raise Sheep

Sheep can be a great choice of livestock to raise on a small farm. They're smaller than other types of farm animals and are relatively simple to take care of, particularly if you plan on raising multiple sheep. If you're planning on getting sheep, you can follow this guide to make sure you do it correctly.

Reasons to Raise Sheep

There are many reasons why you might want to raise sheep. They're great for producing wool, meat, and milk. Unlike some other types of livestock, they can be much easier to care for and manage than animals like cows, pigs, or horses. Sheep can also be useful for the environment. They often help maintain or improve the landscape where they graze. They'll eat weeds along with the grass, which allows other plants to grow better, and their hooves minimize erosion and the compacting of the soil. If you have children, sheep can be a good way to acclimate them to being around farm animals since they're small and very gentle.

Choosing the Right Breed

Before you start raising sheep, you must choose the right breed. Consider your goals. Are you raising them for meat and wool or as a natural lawn care option? Sheep can also yield milk that's used in yogurt and cheese. While there are over 200 different breeds, only a handful are normally kept as livestock. Based on the purpose, they are as follows:

Sheep for Meat and Wool

- Romney (Fleece that's long and glistening)
- Columbia (Large with thick off-white wool)

- Tunis (Mid-sized with cream-colored wool)
- Polypay (Breed often and grow fast)
- Dorset (Mid-sized with thick white wool)
- Corriedale (Large with plenty of meat and high-quality wool)

Sheep for Milk

- Awassi (Shaggy and gentle)

- Lacaune produces excellent
  Milk cheese)
- East Friesian (Produces lots
  of milk)

Sheep for Meat

- Suffolk (Meat popular in the
  United States)
- Katahdin (Low maintenance)
- Hampshire (Very large with
  plenty of meat)

What to Look For when Buying Sheep

When looking for sheep to purchase, there are some things you need to keep in mind. It's best to buy them directly from whoever raised the sheep. This way, you can learn whatever information you need, such as how they were fed and cared for, as well as their history. There are also signs you'll want to look out for when buying sheep that indicate the animal is healthy and will produce good meat, wool, and milk:

- Their eyes should be bright and
  clear.

- They shouldn't be missing any teeth, and the teeth shouldn't be worn down. You also don't want them to have an overbite or underbite.
- Inspect their necks for any swelling or lumps, as this can indicate abscesses or untreated worm infestations.
- Make sure they aren't limping and their hooves have been properly trimmed. Check the other sheep in the flock because if they're limping, it could indicate foot rot, which may infect all the sheep.
- They shouldn't be too fat or too skinny and should have a deep body and wide back. If they have a potbelly, this can indicate that they have a worm infestation.

Even if the sheep you're purchasing "looks" good, it's a good idea to have a vet examine them for any problems that may not be immediately visible. If the vet gives them a clean bill of health, you'll be more confident that you're getting a healthy animal.

Caring for and Feeding your Sheep

Sheep primarily eat fresh grass, hay, and weeds. They can live very well off a diet consisting of grass from pastures, fresh water, salt, and a supplement for vitamins and minerals. A good pasture includes plenty of grass, brush, and trees. For every four sheep, you should have about an acre of land to support them.

During the warmer months, sheep can thrive without the need for supplements, provided they're getting plenty of fresh food. In the colder months or during a drought, you'll have to feed them hay or grain to ensure they're getting all the nutrition they need. Don't leave their food on the ground where it can get dirty or wet. Instead, place it in a raised feeder to keep the hay or grains clean.

Since sheep need more protein in their diet than other grazing livestock, you'll have to feed them a grain supplement to ensure they receive the proper nutrients. This will also need to be done if the pasture where they're grazing doesn't have enough grass or poor-quality grass.

Supplements of vitamins and minerals should be put together specifically for your sheep. You can't use ones meant for other types of livestock, as they often contain high levels of copper, which are toxic to sheep and can prove fatal. They'll also need to be fed salt to prevent bloating - you can give this to them either loose or in granulated form along with their food.

How to Handle Sheep

Sheep are flock animals, meaning they'll usually move towards other sheep when possible. They tend to go uphill or into open spaces and away from buildings or other confined areas. Sheep also flee from anything that startles them, so it's important to keep them away from loud noises or other animals that may make sudden movements.

Using food as an incentive is often the best way for you to train them. They enjoy treats of apples, peanuts, and grain. You can draw them wherever you want by using these treats to get them to follow you –the best way to get them to enter a barn or enclosed space to keep them safe. Because they're gregarious animals, the rest of the flock will instinctively follow if you can get at least one or two sheep to go where you want.

Shearing Sheep

There are two primary reasons that you'll want to shear your sheep: collecting their wool and/or preventing them from overheating in the summer. This means that even if you aren't shearing them for their wool, you'll still need to do so at least once per year. This is generally best performed in the early spring months before the weather becomes too hot. If you have a breed of sheep that grows wool quickly, you may have to shear them at least twice a year.

Make sure you have the proper tools for shearing. Most people choose electric shears since they're easier to use and take less time than doing it the old-fashioned way. Electric shears have three main components: the handpiece, the cutters, and the comb. It's important to make sure the cutters are sharp enough so the tool doesn't tug at the wool and harm the animal. If the blades become too dull, you could try to sharpen them, but it's recommended to buy new cutters for your shearing equipment.

Before you begin shearing, gather your sheep into a pen or fenced-in area, keep them dry, and don't let them eat for a full day ahead of when you'll be shearing them. Get them into the proper shearing position, in which you tip them back and rest their shoulders between your knees to keep them supported. All four of their legs should be in the air with their stomach exposed. Try to keep them as comfortable and calm as possible, which will make the shearing process go smoother. Here are the steps for shearing a sheep:

- Begin with their stomach, as this wool is usually too dirty to be usable, so it will just be discarded. Start from the top of the breastbone and use long, steady strokes downward to the open flank area of the sheep.

- Next, shear the area between the hind legs and crotch. Run the shears up the inside of one leg, then go around the crotch. Of course, be careful when cutting around the udders.

- Turn the sheep 90 degrees and shear the other hind leg, followed by the rear, up to the backbone.

- Change positions again, placing one foot between the sheep's hind legs and the other foot at the base of their spine, holding them securely with your knees. From this position, you can shear their chest, chin, and neck.

- Pull the skintight and shear the sheep's shoulders.

Turn the sheep onto their side so you can shear their back. Start at the tail and make long strokes that run all the way to their head.

- Shear any remaining wool and then collect it, removing any dirty wool or debris before rolling it up.

Congratulations! You've just finished shearing your sheep. Repeat this on any other sheep you have, and they'll be ready to start growing fresh new wool.

How to Raise Goats

Goats are another great animal to raise on a small farm. They can produce large amounts of milk and are relatively simple to handle. You can also use them for low-fat meat. If your farm has any crops, goat manure makes great fertilizer as well. While they require strong fencing and plenty of grazing space, they don't require more effort than other livestock of similar size.

Raising Goats for Milk and Meat

Most female goats can produce up to 90 quarts of milk per month, doing this for ten months every year. This milk can be consumed as regular milk or be turned into cheese, soap, or other dairy-based products. They'll give birth at least once per year, so if you don't intend to have too many, it might be a good idea to get a small number to begin with and expand as new goats are born.

You'll always want at least two goats, so they don't get lonely. If you intend for them to breed, you'll obviously need at least one male and one female. You can use the males for meat after they breed and keep the females for their milk. While goat meat isn't very popular in the

United States, it's quite common in other places worldwide. A single male goat can produce anywhere between 25 to 40 pounds of meat.

Where to House your Goats

You can house your goats in a dry shelter where they'll be protected from the wind and other elements. A three-walled structure should be adequate in most climates, but it's a good idea to keep a small stall that can be used to isolate pregnant goats about to give birth or for when they're sick or injured. Their shelter should consist of packed dirt and wood shavings, hay, or straw for bedding. As hay is one of the primary dietary options for goats, you can use any excess or waste hay for their bedding. Be sure to keep it dry and replace it as needed.

Fencing for Goats

As established, goats require strong fencing since they can knock down or climb over regular types of fences. Even the smallest of holes is enough for them to find a way to escape, so your fence needs to be sturdy and secure enough to prevent this. They won't hesitate to chew through almost anything, including electrical wiring, which is why it's so important to keep them contained. Any sturdy material should suffice, so long as it's at least 5 feet high and cannot be easily broken. Thick wood, chain link, or stock panel fences can all work as a goat fence.

Feeding Your Goats

Most goats eat grass, shrubs, or trees, so having a pasture where they can graze is useful when raising them. Ensure that you rotate where they're grazing to prevent them from overfeeding on a single area, which may kill the grass and allow parasites to grow. They'll also need to be fed additional hay even when they eat while grazing. Goats can consume up to four pounds of hay. Young or pregnant goats require goat feed to ensure they get all the nutrients needed, which you can purchase in premade bags so that all you have to do is give it to them.

Can You Raise Sheep and Goats Together?

While it is possible to raise sheep and goats together, there are some considerations you need to make if you want to take that route. If you're raising them for commercial purposes, this isn't a good idea. However, if you're just raising a small number of them for personal use, *you can absolutely do so.* Caring for a small number of sheep and goats is similar enough that you won't have trouble raising both types of livestock at the same time.

You'll need to make sure both the sheep and goats have had their horns removed if you're raising them together. While they're both generally docile animals, you don't want them goring each other out in the pasture if they become aggressive. That said, as long as you only keep a relatively small number of each, there shouldn't be many issues between them.

Both sheep and goats are grazing livestock, but they prefer different parts of a pasture to feed effectively without conflict over the available supply. When feeding them supplements, it's important to remember to keep them completely separate, though. Goats will need vitamin and mineral supplements that contain copper, which, as stated earlier, is toxic to sheep. Both types of livestock can generally share housing, but if you're using the same fencing, it should withstand the habits of the goats. Sheep will usually respect the boundaries of a fence, but goats will try to escape. If they're both being kept in the same enclosed area, use the strongest type of fencing possible.

When keeping sheep and goats together, the biggest issue is the possibility of disease hopping from one species to the other. You need to have an effective disease prevention plan in place to prevent this. Sheep are more prone to getting internal parasites, but goats can still catch them. Rotating their grazing areas is important for this, as is deworming them. You should also make sure their shelters are dry so they don't end up with foot rot – something both types of livestock are susceptible to.

Ultimately, if you're looking to start raising livestock on your hobby farm, sheep and goats are both great options for beginners. Whether you want to raise them together or choose just one or the other, they offer plenty of benefits. Raising animals can be a very satisfying experience, so if you want to start running a small farm, give sheep and goats a try.

Become a Beekeeper

We've come to the final of this hobby farming book. So far, you've learned about various ways to become self-sufficient and fulfill your hobby farming endeavors. In this , we'll be wrapping up with one of the most interesting activities that will satisfy your sweet tooth and prove essential for supporting the healthy growth of your garden produce.

Here, we'll cover everything there is to know about becoming a successful beekeeper. We'll start with honeybee basics, where and how to get them, then move on to insightful instructions on caring for your hive. Finally, we'll see how to put your DIY skills to the test by building your own beginner's hive. Let's get started!

An Introduction to Honey-Making Bees

From the various bee families we know about today, only one of them can produce honey. Originally from Southeast Asia, the Apis Mellifera is the most common honey-making bee people choose to keep in their home gardens. Famous for their unique social orientation, honeybees exist in colonies with thousands of bee "workers" attending to the needs of their queen. Each worker has their own specific task inside the hive and works around the clock to see it through. If you want to become a good beekeeper, you must learn about your bees' behavior to know when something's off.

The Queen

With one single queen at the center of each hive, its responsibility is to mate and reproduce to build its colony. Typically, the queen bee is inside the hive. However, it does get to go out on special occasions. For instance, when on a mating mission, the queen will leave the hive looking to collect sperm to use from around 80 drones before heading back home, waiting to lay the eggs. You might be surprised to know that it's the queen bee who decides the role of each one of the newborn bees. Using chemical pheromones, the queen exercises its sovereign power over the colony. According to its needs, she will choose which bees act as workers, drones, and which are to become its potential successors. Since there can only be one queen in each hive, potential queens that hatch together will fight to the death for the title.

The Workers

Worker bees are female bees that didn't develop the necessary reproductive characteristics to become queen bees. They're also the busiest bees of all. With tasks ranging from creating new beeswax to building honeycombs to feeding the drones and the queen, workers have many commitments inside and outside the hive. Especially when it comes to honey-making, the worker bees do all of the heavy lifting. They're the ones responsible for mapping the surrounding area to locate nectar and propolis. They also perform pollen packing to make sure it doesn't go bad and infect the entire hive. In addition, worker bees undertake domestic tasks such as cleaning the hive and cooling it off using evaporated water. Since they're the guardians of the hive, worker bees have stingers and can use them to kill off intruders and protect their brood.

The Drones

Drones are the only male bees inside the hive. Their responsibility is to ensure the colony's genetic characters extend to other ones by mating with their queens. Once they fulfill their reproductive mission, male drones die off. However, those who don't succeed return to the hive until the swarming season is over, and worker bees send them off as they become a burden on the hive's resources.

While most people may have a general idea about how honey is made, let's briefly touch base on this fact. This will provide you with all the basics before you can become a beekeeper of your own.

How Bees Make Honey

Bees visit blossoming flowers to suck the nectar using their tongues and then store it in their nectar sacs (different from their stomachs). Once they're back in their hives, they start to pass it to the worker bees, who exchange it from mouth to mouth to thicken its consistency and give it that stickiness honey is known for. The bees then use their wings to fan the excess water from the honey and eventually store it inside honeycomb cells, covering it with a thin layer of beeswax to keep it fresh. By now, you'd think that this intricate process brings out tons of honey. However, the reality is that one honeybee produces a mere tablespoon of honey throughout its lifetime! Doesn't that put things into perspective and encourage you to take this "hobby" seriously? Now that we covered the basics, it's time to get into the practical side of your beekeeping endeavor. How you plan for it will make a world of difference in your experience, from preparing the space you'll need, acquiring your bees and tending to them, and getting all the necessary tools, to important tips on how to build your own hive and avoid getting stung.

Do You Have What It Takes?

Beyond personal readiness, you should first make sure that your home garden is well-equipped for beekeeping and that you own or have access to beekeeping tools. So, before rushing into buying your colony and getting excited about becoming a legitimate beekeeper, here are several considerations to keep in mind.

●**You're Willing to Read and Research the Topic Thoroughly**

Becoming a beekeeper is a huge responsibility, and you cannot start only give up halfway through because it's "too much work." From the very beginning, you have to be honest with yourself and make up your mind about how much time, effort, and resources you're willing to dedicate to this new endeavor. You should also think about how comfortable you are with the idea of getting stung. There's a very high chance you'll be stung at least a few times as a beginner. There's no need to feel discouraged if you find out that you're not completely ready to take this on - there's always next year! So, give yourself enough time to think this through before making a decision.

● **Your Space Allows it**

No matter how eager you are to start beekeeping, you should first make sure you can legally do that and acquire all the necessary licenses.

Besides, it's important to have an experienced beekeeper assess your garden for beekeeping. Do you have a suitable sunny spot to place your hive? Is it accessible enough for you to tend to your hive throughout the year? You don't need to give the idea of beekeeping up if your space isn't ideal.

Instead, try to look for ways to mitigate any space issues that you have.

● You Can Afford Beekeeping

Beekeeping is a long-term and financially demanding commitment, especially at the beginning. Before deciding if you're ready for beekeeping, do some budgeting to evaluate your financial readiness. If you plan on selling your honey, this should be factored in to make this endeavor profitable in the long run. To save up on costs, you can always look for second-hand tools and DIY solutions whenever possible and appropriate.

Essential Supplies

As established, having the essential beekeeping supplies at your disposal is key to get started. As a beginner, you don't need pricey, top-of-the-line tools. Quite the contrary, it's recommended to start simple and then progressively upgrade, as you gain more experience and can handle more complicated tools. Here are the basic tools for a novice beekeeper.

Beekeeper in protective gear
Beehive

You can always purchase a ready-made hive. However, since we've talked about cost-efficiency, it might be a good idea to build your own DIY beehive.

Bee Colony

This will be discussed in detail shortly, giving you a clear idea about where and when to acquire your bees.

Beekeeping Gear

As you'd expect, a special protective beekeeping suit, a mask, and gloves are essential to practice beekeeping safely and efficiently. Of course, there are many options online, but second-hand gear from one of your neighbors will do. As long as it's in good condition and is guaranteed to provide you with the protection you need, of course.

Beehive Smoker and Hand Tools

Beehive Smoker

You'll need a beehive smoker to soothe your bees when tending to them. Other hand tools include items like the scraper to clean any propolis build-up on your hive and the uncapping tool to release honey from the combs.

Honey Extractor

You'll need this tool to harvest honey from the hives. You can go for a manual or a motor-run extractor. Both will do the job, and it's only a matter of preference and readiness.

Building a Beehive

While anyone can build their beehive, simple carpentry skills are required for the best results. Below are a few easy steps you can follow to DIY your hive. 1. Research different types and models of beehives online that are DIY-friendly and well-suited for beginners.

2. Look up multiple sources for a simple step-by-step guide to walk you through the process. Start by purchasing the required material and gathering all the necessary information on cutting and nailing the wooden boards together to make a sturdy, durable beehive.

3. Pay close attention to the details that can make or break your structure. Every corner counts. Otherwise, you'll end up with an awkward and unstable hive.

4. Learn a few tips and tricks on maintaining your new hive spot any structural issues.

5. Finally, make sure you have a clear plan on how you'll be introducing your bees to their new home.

Getting Your Honeybees

You have two main options when buying your bee colony: buy package bees or a nucleus hive. Here are the main differences between the two.

- **Package Bees**: Through a local supplier, you can purchase a package of bees containing worker bees, a separated queen, and a feeder with sugar syrup. Typically, the package comes with all the useful information you need to set up your colony and introduce your workers and queen the right way.

- **Nucleus Hive:** Also known as a "nuc," a nucleus hive is a halfsize colony that you can buy to receive multiple working bees, one queen, and some frames. Although the nucleus hive is a more beginner-friendly option, it carries a bigger risk of spreading disease and bacterial infection throughout your hive.

If you have experience with beekeeping and are willing to try a more daring approach, you can choose to find them in the wild. Besides the obvious difficulty and stinging hazards, there's a good chance you might end up with a defective colony. What's more, there's no guarantee that you'll be able to capture genetically healthy bees that you can rely on to build your colony.

Best Time To Get Your Honeybees

Regardless of the method you opt for, always make sure to consult with the local authorities first and seek professional advice on the best places to purchase honeybees. One more thing to keep in mind when buying your bees is, of course, the timing. Your bees should arrive in early spring to get them set up and ready for the swarming season in time. However, it's best to ask around to find out the best time to place your order and make sure you get the bees on time.

General Tips on How to Care for Your Bees

You've been busy learning about beekeeping, researching how to get your bees, and setting up your colony. Now, it's time to focus on the actual work, namely, caring for your bees. Here are a few general tips on how you can give your bees the best chances to survive, thrive, and provide them with high-quality honey.

Your beekeeping tasks will change every season, as follows:

Spring: Usually the busiest season where you set up new hives and feed your bees to prepare them for the swarming season. You should also check on your queen bee to ensure she's healthy and can carry out its mating duties. It's also a good idea to ensure that your hives have an equal number of bees to keep the balance and provide your bees with the best conditions to go about their duties.

Summer: There isn't much that you can do during the summer - your role will be more about maintaining your hives. You should stop feeding your bees and check on the hives every couple of weeks to ensure there's enough water nearby and that your queen is doing well. It's also the best time to start harvesting your honey (we'll get to this in the next section).

Autumn: In autumn, you'll be busy harvesting your honey, but you'll also need to make sure to leave some aside for your bees to feed on as they prepare for winter. You'll want to scan your hives for any diseases or bacterial infections as well and take appropriate measures as needed. In addition, it's important to maintain good ventilation inside the hives while keeping them protected from strong winds.

Winter: In winter, you want to make sure your hives are well-protected from the cold and that your bees have enough food. There isn't much else to carry on during this season except for keeping your hives in good condition.

Harvesting Honey

We've finally come to the "sweetest" part of beekeeping. The most important thing to bear in mind when harvesting honey is to plan your course of action. Here's how to go about it as safely as possible.

> 1. Wearing your protective gear, gently approach the hive and start using your smoker to calm down the bees before releasing the inner cover with your uncapping tool.

2.   Remove any bees from the way so you can pull out the honey-laden frames and set them aside for extraction.

3.   Using the scratcher, start releasing the wax-sealed honeycomb and place the frame into your honey extractor.

4.   Finally, sift your honey through sheet cloths to get rid of any lingering debris and pieces of wax. Package your honey in clean bottles to keep it fresh and protect it from any contaminants.

As you have seen, beekeeping can be quite a rewarding activity to take on as part of your farming hobby. By now, you may feel a little overwhelmed with all information and ideas discussed so far. Fortunately, the following conclusion will bring everything together so that you have a clear idea of how to start your hobby farming journey.

Conclusion

Regardless of where you reside, there will always be some sort of farming that you can undertake. In fact, so many regions of the world have unique animals or crops, so you can easily turn your hobby into a very profitable niche.

The idea behind showing you all these different avenues of farming is to broaden your perspective and show you how flexible and rewarding farming can be. The essence of hobby farming is to be able to go out to the field and start doing something, anything, with whatever resources are at your disposal. You could choose to incorporate all of the ideas discussed or opt for something else entirely. Keep in mind that these are not the only fields of farming available. If you are interested in any plant or any domestic animal, bird, or fish, chances are it can be farmed. While global principles apply to any type of farming, the real fun begins when you choose to pursue something that you truly enjoy. More than simply a means to generate income and ensure self-sufficiency, farming can be a brilliant way to preserve resources.

In the end, the most valuable asset in your farmer's arsenal is a can-do attitude and a positive mindset to achieve the goals you may have set for yourself. Let's face it: Farming any resource can initially be intimidating and frustrating, particularly if you have no experience working in agriculture. However, farmers aren't rocket scientists. It's one of the oldest occupations on the planet and will certainly be around for quite some time. As is the case with all hobbies, farming is meant to be an enjoyable experience that can provide good returns if you do it right. We hope you enjoy raising whatever you choose to farm and develop your skills as a farmer.